A New True Book

CHILE

By Karen Jacobsen

Flag of Chile

CHILDRENS PRESS®
CHICAGO

A young Chilean farmer
picks potatoes.

Library of Congress Cataloging-in-Publication Data

Jacobsen, Karen.
    Chile / by Karen Jacobsen.
        p.   cm. — (A New true book)
    Includes index.
    Summary: Describes the geography, history, people,
and culture of Chile.
    ISBN 0-516-01111-1
    1. Chile—Juvenile literature. [1. Chile.]
I. Title.
F3058.5.J33   1991
983—dc20
90-20818
CIP
AC

PHOTO CREDITS

The Bettmann Archive—22 (right)

Victor Englebert—13 (left), 36

Gartman Agency/Photri—8

Reprinted with permission of *The New Book of Knowledge,* 1989 edition, © Grolier Inc.—4

H. Armstrong Roberts—© J. Ianiszewski, 17 (left); © K. Scholz, 40

Martin Hintz—31 (right)

Historical Pictures Service, Chicago—19 (right), 20, 22 (left)

© Emilie Lepthien—44 (top left)

Nawrocki Stock Photo—© Carlos Vergara, 4 (top & center); © Mark Gamba, 9

Chip and Rosa Maria de la Cueva Peterson—7, 33 (left), 39 (right), 42

Photri—19 (left), 33 (right)

Reuters/Bettmann—32

Root Resources—13 (right); © Grace Lanctot, 11, 18

Tom Stack & Associates—© Gary Milburn, 44 (bottom)

Stock Imagery/Hillstrom Stock Photo—© A.P.C., 4 (bottom)

SuperStock International, Inc.—© Jorge Ianiszewski, Cover; © Ernest Manewal, 2, 12, 17 (right), 28, 34 (2 photos), 35 (left), 39 (left), 43; © Karl Kummels, 6 (right), 10 (right), 16; © P. Schmidt, 6 (left); © Kurt Scholz, 25, 27 (right), 41; © G. Ricatto, 35 (right); © Joe Barnell, 38; © Hubertus Kanus, 44 (top right)

TSW/CLICK—Chicago—© David Levy, 14

UPI/Bettmann Newsphotos—10 (left), 27 (left), 29, 31 (left)

Valan—© Jean-Marie Jro, 45

Cover: Pachallatas and Parinacota volcanoes near Arica, Chile

TABLE OF CONTENTS

The Nation...5

The Land...7

Northern Chile...11

Central Chile...13

Southern Chile...15

The People of Chile...17

Long Ago in Chile...19

Independence...21

Wars and Battles...24

The Early 1900s...26

Salvador Allende Gossens...29

Democracy Returns...32

Life in Chile...33

Words You Should Know...46

Index...47

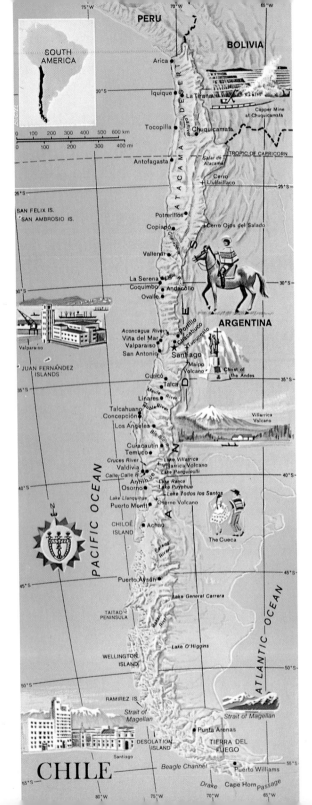

PERU

BOLIVIA

SOUTH
AMERICA

Arica
20°S
Iquique ● La Tirana
Copper Mine
at Chuquicamata

Tocopilla ● Chuquicamata

TROPIC OF CAPRICORN
Salar de
Atacama
Antofagasta ● Cerro
Llullaillaco
25°S   25°S

SAN FELIX IS.
SAN AMBROSIO IS.

Potrerillos ●
Copiapó ● Cerro Ojos del Salado

Vallenar ●   30°S
La Serena ●
Coquimbo ● Andacollo
Ovalle ●

ARGENTINA

Valparaiso

JUAN FERNÁNDEZ
ISLANDS

Aconcagua River
Viña del Mar ● Portillo
Valparaiso ● Caracabuco
San Antonio ● Tupungato
Santiago
Maipo
Volcano   Christ of
the Andes
Curicó ●
Talca ●
35°S   Linares ●   35°S
Maule River
Talcahuano ● Ñuble River   Villarrica
Concepción ●   Volcano
Los Angeles ●
Bío Bío River
Curacautín ●
Temuco ●
Cruces River ● Lake Villarrica
Valdivia ● Villarrica Volcano
Calle-Calle R. ● Lake Panguipulli
Antilhue ● Lake Ranco
Osorno ● Lake Puyhue
Lake Llanquihue ● Lake Todos los Santos
Puerto Montt ● Osorno Volcano
40°S   CHILOÉ ● Achao   40°S
ISLAND
The Cueca
Palena
River
Puerto Aysén ●
45°S   45°S
Lake General Carrera
TAITAO
PENINSULA
Baker River
Lake O'Higgins
WELLINGTON
ISLAND
50°S   50°S
RAMIREZ IS.
Strait of
Magellan   Strait of Magellan
Santiago   Punta Arenas ●
DESOLATION   TIERRA DEL
ISLAND   FUEGO
55°S
CHILE   Beagle Channel ● Puerto Williams   55°S
Drake Cape Horn Passage

The friendly people of Chile

THE NATION

Chile is a long, narrow country on the west coast of South America. From north to south, Chile stretches for 2,650 miles. From east to west, Chile is 236 miles across at its widest point.

Three other nations share borders with Chile. Bolivia and Argentina are in the east, and Peru is in the north. The Pacific Ocean lies along Chile's long western border.

The city of Santiago is the center of government and business in Chile. The congress meets in the Parliament Building (inset).

Chile is a republic. It has a constitution, a congress, and a president. The capital of Chile is Santiago. The language of Chile is Spanish.

THE LAND

Chile has three main landforms: low mountains, a central valley, and high mountains. All three run side by side for the length of the country. The low mountains rise along Chile's Pacific coast. The high mountains

Chile's coastal mountains are between 2,000 and 7,000 feet high.

The Andes Mountains rise to heights of over 20,000 feet along Chile's eastern border.

are in the east, near Bolivia and Argentina. They are part of the Andes Mountains.

The central valley lies between the low mountains and the high mountains. It has a variety of climates. Near Puerto Montt—on the Gulf of Ancud—the central valley is a cool, rainy area covered with trees. But in the far north, near Peru, the valley is a hot, dry desert.

In 1960, and again in 1985, powerful earthquakes struck Chile. Thousands of people were killed.

A ranch in Chile's central valley

Earthquakes are not the only natural dangers in Chile. There are landslides in the mountains, flash floods in the valleys, and tidal waves along the seacoast. Chile also has many volcanoes. Several are active and could erupt at any moment.

The earthquakes of 1960 and 1985 left thousands homeless (left). Villarrica Volcano is in southern Chile (right).

The Andes Mountains as seen from an airplane

NORTHERN CHILE

Steep, fog-covered cliffs
rise up from the ocean along
Chile's northern coast. Far
off in the east, there is snow
on the peaks of the Andes
Mountains.

11

There is no fog, no rain, and no snow in the Atacama Desert. It is the driest desert in the world.

But in the northern part of the central valley, there is almost no water at all. The central valley in northern Chile is called the Atacama Desert. There are deposits of copper and nitrate in the Atacama Desert.

CENTRAL CHILE

More than 85 percent of
Chile's 13 million people live
in the central part of Chile,
south of the Atacama Desert.
This part of the country has
the nation's best farmland and
the most pleasant climate.

Harvesting grapes (left) near Santiago and a small
hillside farm (right) in southern Chile.

Rivers from the high Andes bring water into several small valleys in Central Chile. Fruit and vegetable crops grow very well in the rich soil.

The land between Temuco and Puerto Montt is known as the Lake District.

Water from melting glaciers in the Andes runs down into a dozen large lakes in the Lake District.

SOUTHERN CHILE

The southern part of Chile has mountains, glaciers, and dozens of islands. The islands reach all the way to Cape Horn, at the southern tip of South America.

Chile's southern coast is a wild, windswept area. The weather is almost always stormy, with heavy rains or snow and few sunny days.

Patagonia, a lowland plain, lies in the far south.

Punta Arenas on the Strait of Magellan is a seaport and fishing center. It is the southernmost city in Chile.

Across the Strait of Magellan is Tierra del Fuego, an island that is divided between Chile and Argentina.

Chile's Juan Fernandez Islands lie 400 miles out in the Pacific Ocean. Easter Island lies about 2,400 miles from the mainland.

Stone drawings (left) made by the Araucanians.
Today, five percent of Chile's people are Araucanian (right).

THE PEOPLE OF CHILE

The first people of Chile were Indian tribes of hunters and food gatherers. The largest and strongest tribe was the Araucanian people. They lived south of the Atacama Desert in the central valley.

17

These schoolchildren are descendants of the Indian and European people who settled in Chile.

About two-thirds of all Chileans are *mestizos* — people with both Indian and European ancestry. Most mestizos are part Spanish.

Most of the Spanish settlers came to Chile in the 1800s and later. Other groups of settlers came from England, Ireland, Germany, Italy, and Yugoslavia.

Ruins (left) of an ancient Inca city.
Diego de Almagro (right) and his
men found no gold in Chile,
and almost died in the desert.

LONG AGO IN CHILE

In the 1400s, the Inca people
of Peru built a strong empire.
The Inca warriors conquered
the Indians in northern and
central Chile, and the
Araucanians moved into the
southern part of central Chile.
In 1535, Diego de Almagro

19

Pedro de Valdivia founded the Spanish town of Santiago, which later became Chile's capital.

and some other Spanish soldiers left Peru to look for gold in Chile.

In 1540, Pedro de Valdivia and more Spanish soldiers marched into Chile. Other Spanish settlers soon came to live in Chile. They set up large farms and made the Indians work on the farms as slaves.

INDEPENDENCE

Chile was a Spanish colony for almost three hundred years. In 1810, a group of landowners decided to rule Chile themselves. They declared Chile to be an independent country. Then, in 1814, a Spanish army from Peru recaptured Chile. But the Chilean landowners still wanted to run their own government in Chile.

Bernardo O'Higgins (left) was a great hero in Chile.
O'Higgins and José de San Martín (right) won freedom for Chile.

Bernardo O'Higgins
(1778-1842) was Chile's
first national leader. In 1813,
he went to Argentina and
joined General José de San
Martín, the leader of
Argentina's freedom fighters.
In 1817, San Martín,
O'Higgins, and their army

crossed the Andes into Chile. They fought and defeated the Spanish army.

In 1818, O'Higgins became Supreme Dictator of the new nation of Chile. In 1822, O'Higgins wrote Chile's first constitution. He tried to collect taxes to build roads and schools, but the wealthy landowners did not want to pay. In 1823, the landowners forced O'Higgins to resign and to leave Chile. The landowners took over the government.

WARS AND BATTLES

Chile wanted to take over the rich nitrate deposits in the Atacama Desert, which belonged to Bolivia. So, in 1879, Chile attacked Bolivia and Peru. The fighting was known as the War of the Pacific. Chile won the war in 1883, and the mineral-rich northern desert became part of Chile.

In the 1800s, settlers began to move south of the

Morro de Arica—
the site of a
battle in the
War of the Pacific.

Bío-bío River into Indian
lands. There were many
battles between the Indians
and the newcomers. In 1883,
the Indians were forced to
sign a treaty. They agreed to
live in peace on a reservation.

THE EARLY 1900s

In World War I (1914-1918), Chile sold nitrates—for making gunpowder—to both of the warring sides.

But, when the war was over, the need for so much nitrate was also over. People lost their jobs.

In World War II (1939-1945), Chile again did not take sides. But it sold copper, nitrates, and other supplies to the United States, Britain, and France.

After the war, Chile
continued to develop its
trade with foreign countries.
Many foreign companies
bought mines and set up
factories in Chile. Chile's
wealthy landowners became
part-owners of its businesses.

Copper and nitrate are important mineral resources.
Left: Workers shovel nitrate from evaporation pans.
Right: A copper mine near Arica.

In addition, there was a growing middle class in Chile. Its members included Chile's professional and business people. The middle class wanted more power in Chile's government.

But most of Chile's people were very poor. They could not read or write, and they had to work hard for low pay.

There is still much poverty in Chile. These children live in a Santiago shantytown.

SALVADOR ALLENDE GOSSENS

Salvador Allende Gossens was elected president in 1970.

In 1961, the Chilean government started a 10-year, $10-billion program to rebuild and develop the country's economy.

In 1970, Chileans elected Salvador Allende Gossens as president. Under his leadership, the government took land from the big landowners to sell to farmers with no land. The government also took over Chile's mining industry.

These actions made Chile's upper- and middle-class people very angry with the Allende government. There were strikes and protest marches. Chile's money lost much of its value.

In September of 1973, military troops attacked President Allende and his supporters in the Presidential Palace. There were battles in

Santiago's Presidential Palace (left) was attacked during the 1973 army revolt led by General Augusto Pinochet Ugarte (right).

many Chilean cities. Allende died in the fighting.

The leader of the army attack was General Augusto Pinochet Ugarte. He and three other generals took control of Chile's government. They closed down Chile's National Congress and ignored the people's civil rights.

31

DEMOCRACY RETURNS

President Patricio Aylwin —
before his election in 1989,
Chile had been ruled
by military dictators
for sixteen years.

After many protests by the people of Chile, the military government agreed to allow elections in December 1989. Some people voted for General Pinochet, but most Chileans voted for Patricio Aylwin. He took office as president in March 1990.

LIFE IN CHILE

Today in Chile, the ecomomy is growing. But more than half of Chile's people are still very poor.

In rural areas, many of Chile's poor people live and work on large farms called *fundos*. In the cities, many

The farm workers live in one- or two-room houses (left). A young girl (right) works in the fields.

Some people who live in *callampas* (left) are moving to new government housing projects (right).

poor people live in two- and three-story tenement houses called *conventillos*. Other poor Chileans live in shacks in crowded shantytowns called *callampas*. In contrast, many middle- and upper-class Chileans live in

Modern apartments for the middle class (left).
Chileans (right) visit a Santiago shopping mall.

modern apartment buildings
with electricity and running
water.

Most Chileans wear
modern clothing. Business
people wear suits and
dresses.

Chilean cowboys, called
huasos, have their own

Huasos compete in yearly rodeos. In the picture above,
two riders try to pin a steer against the wall.

special work clothes. Their boots have high heels and big spurs. They wear short, handwoven ponchos called *mantas*. Their flat-topped hats have wide brims that protect their eyes from the sun and rain.

Many of Chile's holidays honor important events in Chile's past. September 18 is Chile's Independence Day. On September 19, Armed Forces Day, there is a big military parade in Santiago.

Most of Chile's people follow the Roman Catholic religion. On Christian holy days, Chileans attend church, eat special foods, and have parties.

Chileans love to sing and dance. Their national dance, the *cueca*, is a lively dance for couples.

Cueca dancers stamp their feet and twirl handkerchiefs above their heads.

Empanadas (left), a favorite Chilean food, are pastries filled with meat or cheese. Fruits and vegetables are sold in Chile's markets (right).

Many Chilean dishes are made from beef, lamb, or fish mixed with vegetables. Chile's poorest people do not have a healthy, well-balanced diet. They eat mainly beans, potatoes, and bread.

All children in Chile are supposed to begin school at age seven.

About 90 per cent of
Chile's people can read and
write. But only a small
number of Chileans attend
high schools and colleges.

Education is free for eight
years of elementary school.
Elementary students study
Spanish, mathematics,

The University of Santiago. Very few of Chile's young people have the education to enter one of Chile's universities.

natural science, social studies, art, and physical education.

But, some children— usually poor children—do not go to school at all. Some live too far from a school,

Chilean high-school girls in uniform. Less than 10 percent of all high-school students graduate from their schools.

and some must go to work every day to help their families.

At age fifteen, students may go on to private high school for four more years of classes.

Futbol—soccer—is Chile's favorite sport.

Boys playing soccer in Santiago. Crowds of people watch professional teams play soccer in stadiums all over the country.

Children play *futbol* before and after school. The Chilean national team has played in World Cup games.

Wealthy Chileans watch or take part in several other sports, such as tennis, skiing, horse racing, golf, and basketball.

Chile's spectacular natural wonders include glaciers (top left),
waterfalls (top right), and majestic mountains (bottom).

The long, narrow country
of Chile holds many different
and amazing features —
volcanoes, glaciers, desert,
high mountain peaks, rich
farmland, and more. Chile is
a truly beautiful land. **45**

WORDS YOU SHOULD KNOW

callampa (kuh • LAHM • pah) — a shantytown built in or near a Chilean city

capital (KAP • ih • til) — the city or place where a country's government meets

congress (KAHNG • gress) — a representative law-making body; a parliament

constitution (kahn • stih • TOO • shun) — a system of basic laws or rules for the government of a country

conventillo (kahn • ven • TEE • yoh) — a building with apartments for many families

cueca (KWAY • kah) — the Chilean national dance; couples stamp their feet and twirl handkerchiefs above their heads

earthquake (ERTH • kwayk) — a sudden violent shaking of the earth, often with cracks appearing

empire (EM • pyre) — a group of nations or peoples united under one ruler

fundo (FOON • doh) — a very large farm or ranch in Chile

glacier (GLAY • sher) — a large, riverlike field of ice

huaso (hoo • WAH • soh) — a Chilean cowboy

landslide (LAND • slyde) — the fall of rocks and earth down the side of a mountain

mestizos (mehss • TEE • soss) — people who are partly Indian and partly another race

nitrate (NY • trayt) — a salt used to make fertilizer and explosives

poncho (PAHN • choh) — a garment that fits over the shoulders and hangs down in front and back

professional (proh • FESH • uh • nil) — people who practice a profession, such as doctors, lawyers, and teachers

republic (rih • PUHB • lik) — a country that has elected officials

reservation (reh • zer • VAY • shun) — land set aside for a group of people to live on

shantytown (SHAN • tee • town) — a neighborhood of small houses or huts built in a crude way

tenement (TEN • ih • mint) — an old, crowded apartment building, especially one in a city slum

tidal wave (TYE • dil WAYVE) — a very high wave that floods the shore, caused by an earthquake or storm at sea

volcano (vahl • KAY • noh) — an opening in the earth's crust through which molten lava, smoke, or steam erupts

INDEX

Allende Gossens, Salvador, 29, 30, 31

Almagro, Diego de, 19

Andes Mountains, 8, 11, 14, 23

Araucanian people, 17, 19

Argentina, 5, 8, 16, 22

Atacama Desert, 12, 13, 17, 24

Aylwin, Patricio, 32

Bio-bio River, 25

Bolivia, 5, 7, 24

callampas (shantytowns), 34

Cape Horn, 15

capital, 6

Central Chile, 13-14

central valley, 7, 8-9, 12, 17

cliffs, 11

climate, 8-9, 13, 15

clothing, 35, 37

congress, 6, 31

constitution, 6, 23

conventillos (tenements), 34

copper, 12, 26

cowboys, 35, 37

crops, 14

cueca (dance), 38

dance, 38

desert, 9, 12, 45

earthquakes, 9, 10

Easter Island, 16

education, 40-42

elections, 32

European settlers, 18, 20

factories, 27

farmland, 13, 45

farms, 20, 33

flash floods 10

food, 39

freedom fighters, 22, 23

fundos (farms), 33

futbol (soccer), 42-43

glaciers, 15, 45
gold, 20
government, 6, 21, 23, 28, 29,
    30, 31
Gulf of Ancud, 8
holidays, 37
housing, 33-35
huasos (cowboys), 35, 37
Inca people, 19
independence, 21-23
Indians in Chile, 17, 18, 19, 20,
    25
islands, 15
Juan Fernandez Islands, 16
Lake District, 14
landforms, 7
landowners, 21, 23, 27, 30
landslides, 10
mantas (ponchos), 37
mestizos, 18
middle class, 28, 30
minerals, 12
mines, 27, 30
mountains, 7, 8, 10, 11, 14, 15,
    23, 45
natural dangers, 9-10
nitrates, 12, 24, 26
Northern Chile, 11-12
O'Higgins, Bernardo, 22, 23
Pacific coast, 7, 10, 11, 15
Pacific Ocean, 5, 11, 16
Patagonia, 16

people of Chile, 17-18
Peru, 5, 9, 19, 20, 21, 24
Pinochet Ugarte, Augusto, 31, 32
poor people, 28, 33, 34, 39, 41-
    42
population, 13
president, 6, 29, 32
Puerto Montt, 8, 14
religion, 38
rivers, 14
San Martín, José de, 22
Santiago, 6, 37
size of Chile, 5
snow, 11, 15
Southern Chile, 15
Spanish colony, 21
Spanish language, 6
Spanish people, 18, 19-20, 21, 23
sports, 42-43
Strait of Magellan, 16
Temuco, 14
tidal waves, 10
Tierra del Fuego, 16
trade, 27
trees, 9
Valdivia, Pedro de, 20
valleys, 7, 8-9, 10, 12, 14
volcanoes, 10, 45
War of the Pacific, 24
water, 12, 14
World War I, 26
World War II, 26

About the Author

*Karen Jacobsen is a graduate of the University of Connecticut and
Syracuse University. She has been a teacher and is a writer. She likes
to find out about interesting subjects and then write about them.*